# Engineers Work with Levers

### Carter Hayn

W9-CPE-067

Rosen
Classroom™
New York

1

Engineers use math and science to solve a problem. Some engineers use a lever to solve a problem. A lever is used to move or lift a heavy load.

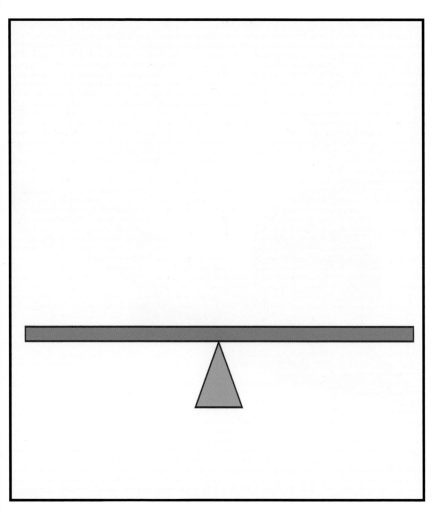

A lever has two parts. The fulcrum is
where the lever pivots. A bar rests on top
of the fulcrum.

Something is placed on one end of the bar. This is called the load. The coin on this lever is the load.

The lever is pushed down on the opposite side of the load. This force is called effort. A large box was put on this lever. It moved the small box up.

Engineers use levers on construction sites. This man moves materials in a wheelbarrow. A wheelbarrow is a lever.

The wheel of a wheelbarrow is the fulcrum. The load goes inside of the wheelbarrow. Effort occurs when someone lifts the handles.

Levers can move heavy materials to high places. The horizontal beam on this crane is a lever. The vertical beam is the fulcrum.

The right side of the beam holds the load. The left side of the beam moves down. The load moves up.

This is a pumpjack. The top of the pumpjack is a lever. The post it rests on is the fulcrum.

This engineer is standing at the fulcrum. The lever moves down and brings oil up from the ground.

# Glossary

**effort**  The force applied to the bar of a lever.

**fulcrum**  The point on which a lever pivots.

**lever**  A bar resting on a pivot, used to move a load.

**load**  Goods or materials placed on a lever.